AROUND
CIRENCESTER
IN OLD PHOTOGRAPHS
FROM THE W. DENNIS MOSS COLLECTION

W. DENNIS MOSS

Photographic Artist

(Under Royal Patronage)

❀

GAINSBOROUGH HOUSE
CIRENCESTER

Telegrams: "DENNIS MOSS, CIRENCESTER"

Telephone No.: 69

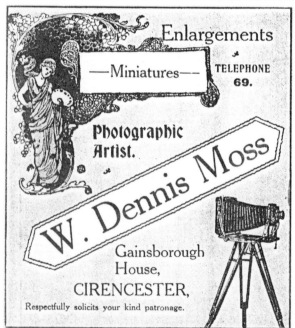

Enlargements

—Miniatures—

TELEPHONE 69.

Photographic Artist.

W. Dennis Moss

Gainsborough House, CIRENCESTER,

Respectfully solicits your kind patronage.

W. DENNIS MOSS ADVERTISE-MENT, c. 1920. These two small advertisements were typical of their era and were used in trade maps of the Cirencester area. They show the services offered by the 'Photographic Artist' who was under royal patronage. Examples of photographs depicting members of the royal family follow later on in the book.

W. DENNIS MOSS ADVERTISE-MENT, 1918.

AROUND
CIRENCESTER
IN OLD PHOTOGRAPHS
FROM THE W. DENNIS MOSS COLLECTION

COMPILED BY
EDWIN CUSS AND PHILIP GRIFFITHS

ALAN SUTTON

Alan Sutton Publishing Limited
Phoenix Mill · Far Thrupp · Stroud · Gloucestershire · GL5 2BU

First published 1991

British Library Cataloguing in Publication Data

Around Cirencester in old photographs.
I. Cuss, Edwin   II. Griffiths, Philip, *1926–*
942.417

ISBN 0-86299-939-1

Front Cover Illustration:
CASTLE STREET, C. 1925. A unique photograph by W. Dennis Moss. On the right are his own
photographic studios at Gainsborough House which he took over from Mortimer Savory just
after the turn of the century. The car belonged to W.D.M. and he used it to tour round the
surrounding area when he was out taking his photographs.

Typeset in 9/10 Korinna.
Typesetting and origination by
Alan Sutton Publishing Limited.
Printed in Great Britain by
The Bath Press, Avon.

CONTENTS

W. DENNIS MOSS, ARPS, FIBP.

W. DENNIS MOSS AND HIS WIFE, C. 1910. Dennis Moss and his wife Catherine are seen here in a Martini car.

INTRODUCTION

WILFRED DENNIS MOSS (1880–1948) ARPS, FIBP

Wilfred Dennis Moss was the fifth of six sons of the late Edward Moss of Cecily Hill, Cirencester. On leaving school he became apprenticed to F. Mortimer Savory, also of Cirencester; from there he went to the firm of E.W. Savory (Mortimer's brother), Fine Arts Publishers, of Bristol.

It was during his time at Bristol that Dennis Moss, making full use of the popularity of postcards, started taking the many photographs from which his picture postcards were printed and sold, naming them the 'Cecily' series after Cecily Hill where he was born. He used some of the more popular and up-to-date subjects of Mortimer Savory, and also spent working holidays along the south coast, photographing scenes at Hastings, Torbay, Penzance and elsewhere, producing postcards of those popular seaside resorts. The bulk of his work was concerned with Cirencester and the south Cotswolds, though coverage was by no means comprehensive, dictated probably by the need to produce what would sell and to keep off other local photographer's territories.

Dennis Moss not only produced postcards, he did the usual portraits, wedding groups, houses etc. An early advertisement of his says:

> Speciality Pictures of children for Christmas Presents. Early sittings are respectfully solicited to avoid disappointment. Studios open from 9:00 a.m. until dusk, Thursdays till 1:00 p.m. General reduction in prices.

His work was much in demand also from the editors of such magazines as the *Tatler* and *Country Life,* among which is a series of pictures of some of the Oxford colleges. Such was his attention to detail that he would climb a pair of steps to get close-ups of some of the finer points of the building. One speciality was polo, which included the visits of the Indian Maharajahs' teams at Westonbirt. On another occasion, in the 1930s, he made a special trip to Belgium to photograph the game there.

He was also a well known photographer of royalty, especially of Queen Mary during her wartime stay at Badminton, as well as other members of the royal family who visited the Duke of Beaufort over the years. Closer to home, the Earl of Bathurst's residence and estate of Cirencester Park were much photographed by him, as was the Abbey House and gardens, home of the Chester-Master family.

Dennis Moss played his part in the life of Cirencester; among his interests were membership of the Cirencester Weavers Company, the Bull Club and the Cirencester Society in London. He was a member of the freemasons, Cotteswold Lodge, and was Worshipful Master in 1918. Kelly's Directory of 1914 says, 'Cirencester Entertainment Company, W. Dennis Moss, Secretary'.

In October 1947 he retired after a lifetime spent as a professional photographer, and, sadly, he died in the following year.

The business was then taken over by George Roper, who moved to Dyer Street, Gainsborough House, where Moss had had his photographic studios, having been sold to a bank. Today's successors are Abbey Studios who hold the remaining stock of W. Dennis Moss negatives.

We had considerable difficulty in deciding how to portray the many villages around Cirencester photographed by W. Dennis Moss. The Roman roads crossing the area, Ermin Street and the Fosse Way, meet at Cirencester, dissecting the area into four, and it was the pattern they provided that we eventually settled on.

All the photographs used in this volume are, to the best of our knowledge, the work of W. Dennis Moss, without whose expert photography there would have been no book.

SECTION ONE

Cirencester

A WEDDING GROUP, 1947. Along with the issue of postcards and the commissioned works, wedding photography was one of the mainstays of photographic work. This picture shows the wedding at Cirencester parish church of Joffre Lock and Gwen Whincup on 15 February 1947. Joffre Lock was from the family of bakers in Watermoor Road and Gwen Whincup was from Welling in Kent. Gwen had worked in London during the war, but because of the bombing her firm was evacuated and relocated in Cirencester where she subsequently met and later married Joffre.

THE CHURCH from the Abbey Grounds, 1908.

THE GATE OF THE ABBEY OF ST MARY, 1908. Both views show the heavy and unseasonal snowfall of 25 April in that year and both views are virtually unchanged to this day. The top view shows the north side of the parish church of St John the Baptist, while in the lower view the Norman gateway of the Abbey is the only visible remains left today of the Augustinian Abbey founded in 1117 by Henry I.

CASTLE STREET, C. 1910. A busy Edwardian scene looking towards the Market Place with the church tower looming high over the roof of the buildings of 1897, now occupied by the post office. Note the fine display at the ironmongers on the right. The small, white shop awning in the centre shades the window display of the W. Dennis Moss studio.

THE MARKET PLACE, 1915.

THE MARKET PLACE, 1915. In the top view are the business premises of Bishop's Family Grocers Store and of J.J. Boulton, both of which were demolished in order to build the new premises of the London City & Midland Bank Ltd. The bank was operating from temporary offices at 4 Black Jack Street. Interestingly a small group of soldiers are standing on the corner by the Bell. In the lower view the ladders can be seen against the building on the right and shop front alterations are being made to Stead & Simpson's, the Family Boot Makers.

THE JUBILEE LAMP, C. 1935. The lamp erected by the people of Cirencester to commemorate the Silver Jubilee of George V. It originally stood on a small traffic island by the police station at the end of Castle Street but, following alterations to the road junction, the lamp was moved to its present site in Dyer Street.

THE MARKET PLACE, c. 1880. This photograph of the church with a carefully posed group of children around the central gas lamp and pump was issued by W.D. Moss, but is mostly probably a photograph by Mortimer Savory whose business he took over in 1904. Today this scene remains one of the most photographed views in the town, especially as seen here with the full midday sun shining on the south side of the Market Place.

CIRENCESTER GRAMMAR SCHOOL, 1904. These buildings were erected in 1880, in New Road which later became Victoria Road in 1887, for use by the Grammar School boys. The girls from the High School later moved into the premises in 1904. Today these buildings house the County Infants and Junior Schools.

THE GRAMMAR SCHOOL GIRLS, C. 1904. It is thought that this is the group of girls from the High School who moved to the Grammar School premises in 1904. The photograph was taken in the quadrangle at the rear of the main buildings and includes female members of staff, and a few small boys.

OLD GRAMMARIANS CRICKET TEAM, 1931. The Old Grammarians *v* The School at cricket was an annual match, and shown in this team photograph which was taken in front of the pavilion is W.R. Hammond, the renowned batsman, who later captained Gloucestershire in 1939 and 1946, and also England in 1946. Back row: E.A. Jefferies, umpire, E. Tranter, S.H. Cole, C. Rumbol, W.O. Rich, P. Bowley, A.T. Tyrell, T. Frazer, umpire. Front row: R.W. Jefferies, A. Leadbetter, W.L. Neale, W.R. Hammond, captain, F.W. Mills, F. Miles.

CRICKET IN CIRENCESTER PARK. A photograph taken early in the century of a match in progress on the cricket pitch up in the Park. The club was formed in 1842 and still plays at this ground. The original pavilion shown in the background is still used, and the club celebrates its 150th anniversary in 1992.

CIRENCESTER (THURSDAY) PHOENIX CRICKET XI, 1905. This group played cricket on their half day off on Thursdays because they all probably worked in the shops in the town and would have had to work all day Saturday.

CIRENCESTER TOWN FOOTBALL XI, 1911. The team shown here are the winners of Stroud and District League 1910/11.

THE MARKET PLACE AND DYER STREET, C. 1880. The two premises on the right, Burrow's Corn & Sack Stores and the arched buildings, previously the Bull Inn, were demolished so that the Bingham Library, designed by V.A. Lawson and founded by Daniel George Bingham, could be built in 1904.

THE BINGHAM LIBRARY, C. 1910. The library was officially opened on 21 September 1905 when a ceremony was held in the Market Place. It is thought that the two trenches that have been dug in the road in front of the imposing facade of the building are for new water mains and sewerage pipes.

THE TOWN HALL, 1909. The Town Hall was housed in the great three-storeyed porch that was added to the front of the church just prior to 1500. This view of the interior of the hall was probably taken following the restoration of the proch in 1909 by F.W. Waller.

REGENT HOUSE, WEST MARKET PLACE, C. 1920. These premises were previously known as Old London House but were renamed Regent House and occupied by French & Sons, Drapers, Hosiers, Milliners and Costumiers. Today it is occupied by Regent Fabrics, but is still known to many local people as 'French's'.

4th Batt. Glo'ster Regiment. Recruits Church Parade.

CECILY HILL, 1904. A view taken from the roof of the Barracks looking down the hill as a Recruits Church Parade of the 4th Battalion Gloucestershire Regiment comes back to its quarters. The Barracks, also known as the Armoury, was built in 1856–7 to house the North Gloucestershire militia.

THE SWIMMING BATHS, 1906. A good view of the mid-Victorian-built open-air swimming pool complete with changing cubicles and rest area.

THE GOLF CLUB, C. 1910. This is the clubhouse that was set up in 1910 when the club moved to their new course close to Baunton alongside the Cheltenham road. Their original course was at Park Corner out by Sapperton, where they had been established since 1893.

POLO IN CIRENCESTER PARK, c. 1900.

POLO IN CIRENCESTER PARK, c. 1904. The Cirencester Park Polo Club was established in the summer of 1894. The top view shows a late Victorian scene at the original Ivy Lodge Ground in the Park. It is thought possible that the temporary enclosure for the members with its seats and marquees was set out for the County Cup matches. The lower view shows some action during a match with one of the two umpires on a horse to the right and the goal judge behind the goal posts. Today the club has other grounds both within the Park and the surrounding area, and practice chukkas, matches and tournaments are played on a regular basis and throughout the season from May until September.

THE COTTAGE HOSPITAL, 1913. The hospital was built by the Earl Bathurst in memory of his first wife, but now the buildings stand empty as the hospital has moved to a new site.

THE MEMORIAL HOSPITAL, C. 1925. This was situated opposite the Cottage Hospital and was converted by V.A. Lawson in 1919 from an old chapel building in memory of the dead of the First World War. It is impressive with its classical columns and this annexe to the hospital was recently restored and remains in use with the health authority.

THE MEAD, 1938. These individually styled houses were started in 1933 on spare land alongside Mead House in Thomas Street. This view is looking back out of the residential cul-de-sac towards the town centre.

M. Salmet. (Daily Mail) at Cirencester.

AVIATOR M. SALMET, 1912. Various aviators visited Cirencester to give flying displays and French pilot M. Salmet is shown landed alongside Grove Lane on 26 June 1912. Pictured with him are the Dugdale family.

Mr. Gustav Hamel. At Cirencester.

AVIATOR MR GUSTAV HAMEL, 1913. German pilot Gustav Hamel is being held back while revving his engine prior to take off for his display in 1913.

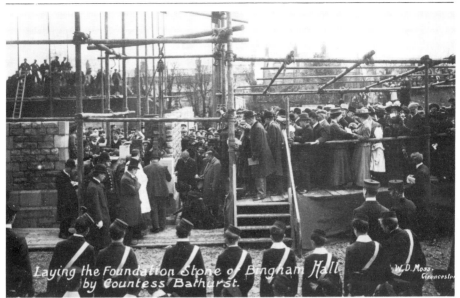

THE BINGHAM HALL, 1908. The Countess Bathurst performed the ceremony of laying the foundation stone of the hall on 7 March 1908. The hall was the gift to the town of Mr D.G. Bingham and it was linked to Watermoor Road by the construction of King Street in the same year. Note the wooden scaffolding tied with ropes and the wealth of details in the crowd gathered for the occasion.

MISSIONARY EXHIBITION, 1926. The Bingham Hall was used to stage a Church Missionary Exhibition. Various displays of their activities and other fund-raising ideas filled the hall and many of them had connections with the Empire in places such as Burma and India.

THE WAGGON AND HORSES INN, c. 1915. This small public house stood in London Road and was a favourite stopping place for local carriers. A typical two-horse covered waggon stands outside. The billboards behind the horses announce the North Cerney Show, a Furniture Sale by Ovens and Son at the Corn Hall, and a visit by Ginnetts No. 1 Circus who were set up in a meadow in the Watermoor Road.

THE QUERNS, 1913. This house was designed and built by P.F. Robinson in 1826 in a Cotswold/Tudor style for Charles Lawrence. It takes its name from the Querns area around the quarries from which the Romans took some of their stone to build the town of Corinium. The house, which was formerly the maternity home, now finds itself isolated within the new hospital complex, and is cut off from its long driveway and lodge by the new dual carriageway road which was realigned up Tetbury Hill out of the town.

WATERMOOR HOUSE, 1912. This house was built in 1826 by W. Jay. The extension on the right was added in the nineteenth century. In later years it became St Michael's school and today it is a private home for elderly people run by the Gloucestershire Old People's Housing Society. The extensive gardens and grounds have now become the St Michael's playing fields.

THE TOWN STATION, C. 1924. A delivery of International tractors was made to Aubrey Rees & Sons by the Great Western Railway to the town railway station. Aubrey Rees, agricultural engineers, had large premises in Spitalgate Lane, but the site is now occupied by the St Johns Meadow development.

AUBREY REES & SONS FORGE, C. 1930. This shows the blacksmith's forge and the workshop where repairs were made to agricultural machinery. On the left is Mr Angel.

CIVIL WAR PAGEANT, C. 1930. This picture remains a mystery as neither the occasion or the location have yet been identified. From the costumes being worn the Civil War theme seems most likely, but if anyone can help with this picture we would be most grateful to hear from them.

QUEEN MARY. This is one of W.D. Moss's royalty photographs and its shows Queen Mary at a factory or warehouse display showing the various meat products of Harris's of Calne. As with the previous picture the location and date have yet to be identified.

THE FIRE AT BARTON MILL, 1923. A disastrous fire completely destroyed Barton Mill on 21 September 1923. The buildings were so badly damaged that they had to be demolished and in this picture the chimney is being brought down. At the time of the fire the mill was being used by Townsends to mill animal feedstuffs and the damage was estimated to be around £20,000.

OXEN PLOUGHING, c. 1930. Oxen were employed on Earl Bathurst's estate at Cirencester and were the last working oxen in the area. They were used for a variety of purposes and a team of six are shown here, probably at a ploughing match judging by the marquee and crowds in the background.

VWH CIRENCESTER HOUNDS, c. 1910. The pack is seen here out in the open park for exercise. Their kennels, which were situated just inside the Park at the top of Tetbury Hill, can be seen in the background.

MILITARY CAMP, 1915. During the First World War the Warwickshire Yeomanry camped and trained in Cirencester Park in the area surrounding the Queen Anne monument. The large tented camp held many hundreds of men and their horses and equipment, and this picture shows hay for the horses being delivered on two large waggons.

POLICE PARADE, C. 1925. The occasion of the parade in Castle Street headed by these ranks of police is uncertain but note Farrell's shop. It sold cycles, accessories, motor cycles and petrol, in spite of being next door to Bridges Garage. Farrell's shop later changed more towards engineering supplies and ironmongery, but it has now been demolished. The name lives on in Farrell Close, the pedestrian precinct leading off Castle Street at this point.

VISIT OF KING GEORGE V TO THE ROYAL AGRICULTURAL COLLEGE, 1923. The visit by the king to the College was made on a very wet day and the parade in the Market Place, which was headed by the Church Lads Brigade band of bugles and drums, were so soaked that all but one of the drum skins split. Note the shops decorated with crests and flags. From the left these shops are Hamper & Fry, Griffiths, Harmers, Stradlings with the town time clock, Gifford & Groves, Walter Hawes, Bailey & Woods and Dale Forty. The visit enabled the king and queen to inspect the College after its recent refurbishment and alterations. Large crowds of people and school children lined the way from the station up Tetbury Hill to the College entrance. At the College the king and queen were shown round the premises by the Principal, Mr Dunstan. After the visit lunch was taken with the Earl and Countess Bathurst at Cirencester Park, then in the afternoon they made a tour round some of the streets of Cirencester before eventually leaving on their train at 3.10p.m.

ROMAN TOMBSTONE. A large limestone block was found at Watermoor in 1836 depicting a Roman cavalryman raising his lance over his fallen enemy. It is known as the Genialis tombstone and is on permanent display in the Corinium Museum. The inscription translates as follows:

Sextus Valerius Genialis, trooper of the Cavalry Regiment of Thracians, a Frisian tribesman, from the troop of Genialis, aged forty, of twenty years service, lies buried here. His heir had this set up.

CORINTHIAN CAPITAL. This figured limestone capital was found at Watermoor in 1838 and later erected in the grounds of the Abbey. Various explanations of its origins and meaning have been put forward, and it seems most likely that it surmounted a sacred column. It is now on permanent display in the Corinium Museum.

THE CORINIUM MUSEUM, c. 1930. This private museum was built by Lord Bathurst in 1856 and was known originally as the Museum of Roman Antiquities, and situated almost opposite the old police station in Park Lane. In 1938 a new museum was opened in Abberley House, and the Bathurst and Cripps families presented their private collections to it.

THE BACON FACTORY, c. 1910. The Cole & Lewis bacon factory was built around 1860 and was finally demolished in 1969. It was between Mount Street and Cotswold Avenue, on the site which is now Martin Close. This small International lorry was part of the transport for the factory.

THE CHURCH AND GOSDITCH STREET, 1880.

THE CHURCH FROM THE NORTH, c. 1904.

THE CHURCH FROM THE ABBEY GROUNDS, 1908.

THE CHURCH FROM ST JOHN STREET, 1913. These four views of the church of St John the Baptist show the alterations that have taken place in the last 110 years, with whole blocks of buildings being demolished to the north of the church. An interesting detail is the infant Cedar of Lebanon tree and in the lower right view the use of St John Street, some twenty-five years after Black Jack Street had been declared its official name.

41

A DELIVERY LORRY, C. 1910. This International lorry was supplied to A.H. Buncombe & Co., wholesale and retail ironmongers, whose premises were in Cricklade Street.

AN INTERNATIONAL ADVERTISEMENT, C. 1910. These three International lorries for local Cirencester firms were taken up Cecily Hill to be photographed lined up outside the Barracks. Aubrey Rees held the dealership for International and these lorries were for A.H. Buncombe & Co., Bridges Garage Ltd, with the right-hand model as yet unlettered.

THE BARRACKS AND PARK ENTRANCE, c. 1910.

Entrance to Earl Bathurst's Park, Cirencester.

THE PARK ENTRANCE, c. 1930. In the top view are the Barracks built just outside the Park gates in 1857 as the armoury for the North Gloucestershire Militia. Note the old cannon behind the railings and one of the two lodges that are to each side of the gates. Inside the Park was a small wooden hut used as a shelter by someone who watched over those entering the Park. In the lower view the ornamental gates that were brought from Carshalton in 1866 can be fully appreciated. Note that at this later date there are two artillery pieces to either side of the gates just inside the Park. This view remains almost identical today.

THE WOODHOUSE IN CIRENCESTER PARK, c. 1904.

THE EWE PEN COTTAGES, 1903. These cottages were thought to be alongside the old road from Cirencester to Bisley and Stroud, which came up Cecily Hill to emerge from the Park at Park Corner. The road was finally closed in 1814 when the new road to Stroud was made from the Tetbury Road and down Kill Devil Hill. This cottage, which may have been a toll house on the old road, has long since been demolished.

Northleach to Cricklade

NORTHLEACH CHURCH, C. 1910. The church of St Peter and St Paul has a most beautiful porch, and is one of the great Cotswold 'wool' churches. It was entirely rebuilt in the mid-fifteenth century with the wealth of wool merchants. Inside the church is a series of brasses to these merchants and their families.

A Part of Northleach.

VIEW THROUGH NORTHLEACH, c. 1905.

The Market Place Northleach.

NORTHLEACH MARKET PLACE, 1911. These two views looking east and west through the town are both across the northern side of the Market Place. In the top view are the Union Hotel and Red Lion Inn on the left with the single row of GPO telegraph poles coming through the town along the route of the main road from South Wales to London. In 1907 these poles were doubled to carry the much increased wire traffic and they are shown in the lower view with white painted slats nailed to them to increase their visibility for traffic.

THE PRISON, NORTHLEACH, 1908. This crossroads of the Fosse Way and the Cheltenham-to-Oxford road became the site of a house of correction in the 1780s. Inside its high walls the cell blocks were designed around a yard with the house for the keeper in the centre. After 1857 the buildings on the site were converted to include a police station and magistrates' court which was in use until 1974. Today the remaining buildings on the site are used by the Cotswold Countryside Collection to house a museum of rural life. In the photograph, as with other pictures of this location, there are always people waiting at the crossroads. Note also the large pile of Cotswold building stone on the right.

General View of Fosse Bridge,
Ghedworth.

FOSSEBRIDGE, 1912. The Fosse Way from Cirencester to Northleach drops steeply down to the small community grouped round the bridge over the River Coln. Modern traffic makes this a dangerous place today, far removed from the tranquil scene shown here.

FOSSEBRIDGE POST OFFICE, C. 1925. The bridge over the river is in the foreground and the post office is the end house with the two dormer windows. The small side road between the houses to the right goes to Coln St Dennis and eventually to most other villages along the Coln valley.

FOSSEBRIDGE HOTEL, 1904. This was a very convenient stopping place along the road for coaches, cars and cyclists, and was also a beautiful location. The buildings have undergone many alterations and enlargements, but it has all been in keeping with the Cotswold style.

FOSSEBRIDGE HOTEL GARDENS, 1904.

Fosse Bridge Hotel from Gardens.

FOSSEBRIDGE HOTEL GARDENS, C. 1925. In the top view the gardens to the rear of the buildings have been carefully tended in true Edwardian style so that lawn tennis can be played. Some twenty years later a gardener still tends the lawn and tennis court with the help of a small pony to pull the heavy and wide mower.

THE APPROACH TO BARNSLEY, 1905. This is the road from Cirencester as it curves sharply into the village. The village remains a well-preserved Cotswold community with hardly any modern alterations out of context. Barnsley Park which lies off the road out of the village towards Bibury is a fine house of the later Renaissance period.

BARNSLEY RECTORY, C. 1912. This house was built in 1697, but was altered in the 1830s. It served as the rectory from 1762 to 1932.

Ablington Manor.

ABLINGTON MANOR, 1905. This shows the Manor facing out into the grounds with the River Coln in the foreground. The Manor was built in 1590 by John Coxwell and towards the end of the nineteenth century it became the home of J. Arthur Gibbs whose book, *A Cotswold Village*, published in 1898, was one of the early books to describe the Cotswold way of life.

ARLINGTON MILL, 1905. The mill, seen here from the Swan Hotel gardens, probably dates from the seventeenth century and may well be on the site of a much earlier mill. It was originally water-powered but was later steam-powered and was used for a cloth mill and later as a corn mill. The cottage in the front was added at the end of the seventeenth century, while alterations and strengthening to the mill in the nineteenth century also required buttresses. W.D. Moss issued the same view later on and attempted to erase the mill chimney possibly thinking it would give the picture more appeal.

VIEW FROM BEHIND THE SWAN HOTEL AT BIBURY, C. 1935. The hotel is on the left, while its gardens were on the opposite side of the road. They were very popular as tea gardens, but as yet the village is not besieged with tourists and cars. In the centre of the picture lies the large open expanse of Rack Island.

SWAN HOTEL GARDENS, C. 1920. The trout hatchery buildings are to the left and the stream on the right was from a spring that delivered up to five million gallons of water per day which was sufficient to drive a waterwheel in the small shed. This waterwheel pumped water to various houses in Bibury.

THE RIVER COLN AT BIBURY, 1938. These fishermen are fishing for trout from Rack Island, but the sender of the postcard remarked 'Weather perfect, in fact too good for fishermen'.

ARLINGTON ROW, 1938. These cottages which may have originally been a fourteenth-century wool warehouse must now be one of the most photographed locations in the Cotswolds. The view remains basically unchanged and the tail race from Arlington Mill has just been dredged out.

PIGEON HOUSE FARM, BIBURY, 1937. The cottage on the left is thought to be from the fifteenth century, while the round dovecote giving the farm its name is typical of many such buildings around the Cotswolds.

COLN ST ALDWYNS MANOR HOUSE AND CHURCH, 1912. The church of St John the Baptist has Norman remains, but was severely restored in mid-Victorian times. It lies close to the sixteenth-century manor house which, after centuries as a farmhouse, was restored and altered in 1896 by Sir Michael Hicks-Beach who was chancellor of the exchequer at the time.

The Post Office, Coln St. Aldwyns.

COLN ST ALDWYNS POST OFFICE, 1905. The village postman stands outside the post office at the top end of Coln Street with two typical Edwardian ladies. Note the oil lamp, several of which were placed round the village, and also the single telegraph line coming into the post office.

COLN ST ALDWYNS SHOP, 1905. This view at the top of the street shows the crossroads and the village chestnut tree. The shop was the Coln Co-operative Society Ltd and this postcard was made for and sold only by this shop as one of their own series.

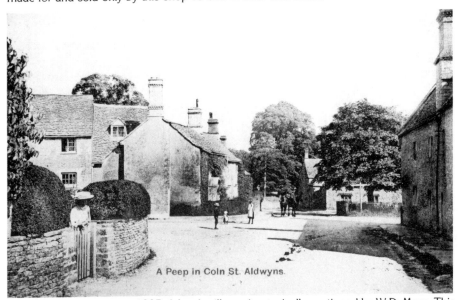

A PEEP IN COLN ST ALDWYNS, 1905. A lovely village view typically captioned by W.D. Moss. This shows another angle on the crossroads, in this case straight on for Hatherop, left to Bibury or right to Quenington. The tree on the island surrounded by railings is naturally now much bigger and recently village meetings were held under its branches to campaign for the restoration of the village public house, the New Inn, which had been closed for development.

COLN, HATHEROP AND QUENINGTON BRANCH OF THE BRITISH LEGION, 1939.

COLN, HATHEROP AND QUENINGTON HOME GUARD, 1941. To talk of Coln is also to talk of Hatherop and Quenington, known collectively as CHQ. For certain occasions the three villages have always come together and here are two official wartime photographs for which film was available. In the top view of the British Legion Lord St Aldwyn is seated in the centre in uniform while the lower shows the combined group of the Home Guard.

HATHEROP, looking east, 1905.

HATHEROP, looking west, 1905. These two views are of the same street taken on the same day. In the top view the base of the village cross can be seen to the left, while in the lower view the arched entrance to Hatherop school is on the left. Most of the cottages in the village belonged to the Estate.

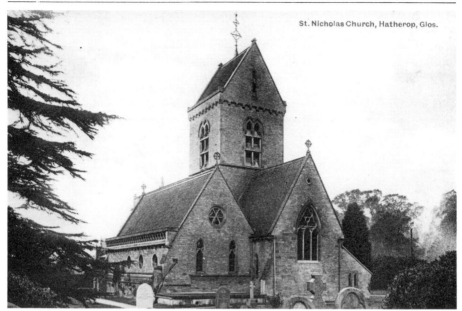

St. Nicholas Church, Hatherop, Glos.

HATHEROP CHURCH, C. 1920. The church of St Nicholas was almost completely rebuilt in 1855 at the expense of Lord de Mauley who commissioned Henry Clutton to do the work. The result was a building in the French – Gothic style somewhat alien to the Cotswolds.

HATHEROP CASTLE, C. 1920. The original Elizabethan house was rebuilt in the early 1850s by Henry Clutton for Lord de Mauley. The alterations included a battlemented porch and tower giving it the appearance of a castle. It was then purchased by the Bazley family in 1867, but today it is Hatherop Castle School.

QUENINGTON, 1904. This is a lovely village scene by the Pound at the top of Front Street with Back Street off to the left. Behind the pony and trap is the Keepers Arms, one of the three pubs in the village at the time. The road runs down into the valley of the River Coln where a preceptory of the Knights Hospitallers was founded in 1193, and the tall fourteenth-century gatehouse is the only remaining feature today.

QUENINGTON POST OFFICE, 1904. A small shop and post office operated from this old cottage in Bottom Road.

QUENINGTON CHURCH, 1904. Th church of St Swithin is down by the River Coln and although it was subjected to drastic internal and external restoration in 1882 when the bellcote and west window were added, it still has Norman features of the twelfth century. The north and south Norman doorways are especially rich, and really must be seen and studied to be appreciated.

EASTLEACH, 1909. The twin villages of Eastleach Martin and Eastleach Turville are divided by the River Leach. In the background is the road bridge, and then the stone clapper footbridge known as Keble's Bridge where once people dipped out water in buckets before the piped supply was installed to the carved stone outlet on the right. To the left is the church of St Andrew which has many Norman features and Bridge Cottage stands in the centre.

FILKINS VILLAGE, C. 1920. The scene is full of children, perhaps going home from school. The post office is on the left with three lines on the telegraph poles. The Lamb Inn, selling 'Hall's Noted Ales and Stout', is on the right.

Id Houses, Burford.

BURFORD HIGH STREET, 1912. Captioned 'Old Houses' by W.D. Moss, the steep High Street certainly had an assortment of styles. The shops, from the right, are believed to be Sharp and Son shoes, L. Lomas family butcher, in London House Akerman family grocers and provisions merchant, G. Packer printing office and bookseller, the Bull Hotel, Hambidge grocer, and the last that can be made out is Thomas house furnishers.

THE BULL HOTEL, BURFORD, 1915. This was an old coaching inn and is the only red-brick building in Burford High Street. At one time the premises to the left were used as an annexe to the hotel. To the right is the shop of G. Packer with two boards advertising Burford postcards and a book called *Story of Burford*.

THE TOLSEY, BURFORD, 1912. An old building in the High Street that has had many uses. Perhaps originally a market house with open shelter for stalls underneath, and later filled in and used to house the horse-drawn manually pumped fire engine. It is now used by the parish council and the museum.

Sheep Street, Burford.

SHEEP STREET, BURFORD, 1912. This street with its wide grass banks was used for the market, when sheep and animals were penned in with hurdles on the grass. It was also used for the Burford mid-summer hiring fair where once a year people could offer themselves for employment, mainly in agriculture.

Burford Cottage Hospital.

BURFORD COTTAGE HOSPITAL, 1907. This was built in 1902 by Thomas H. Cheatle. It had four beds for men and four beds for women with one small private room. The matron's accommodation was upstairs.

LECHLADE HIGH STREET, 1911. The New Inn stands on the south side of the large triangular shaped Market Place. This view looking down the High Street towards Fairford had at least five public houses in it and the large overhanging tree on the right grew in the front garden of Davis the Chemist, who was also the professional photographer in Lechlade and the district for many years.

OTTER HOUNDS MEET AT LECHLADE, 1912. These otter hounds hunted either up and down the River Leach or up and down the River Coln and they always seemed to start or finish at a hotel or public house for refreshments before and after the event. Note the notice boards on the left on the wall of the police station and the saddle maker's shop to the right.

THE NEW INN, LECHLADE, c. 1935. A rarely seen view of the unchanged mid-eighteenth-century hotel from its yard at the back showing the arched entrance for the coaches in the days before the turn of the century. The distinctive different-coloured bricks also show up well with the view through the arch to the Market Place.

ON THE RIVER THAMES AT LECHLADE, 1904. At the rear of the New Inn the meadow stretched down to the river and here the hotel had a small landing stage. Prior to the wharf being opened to pleasure boats they tied up here and most likely made use of the hotel which offered 'Good Accommodation for Boating Parties'.

LECHLADE HIGH STREET, c. 1910. This is the road from Fairford and on the left is the Labourer's Arms selling 'Bowlys Entire Beers'. By the pavement is one of the lion-faced water taps, manys of which were installed around the streets for people to get water from. Looking into the Market Place the spire of the church of St Lawrence shows above the houses. This spire has always been a most conspicuous landmark for miles around the town in the flat Thames valley countryside.

LECHLADE WATER CARNIVAL, C. 1910. The carnival was held on August Bank Holiday Monday for many years and all events took place on the river. Here the competitors in a swimming event are lined up on a pontoon moored in the river, while a good crowd watches from the banks and from the eighteenth-century Halfpenny Pike Bridge. Note the wooden platforms to the left where the diving events took place into the deeper part of the river just below the bridge.

St. John's Lock, Lechlade. No. 2.

ST JOHN'S LOCK, LECHLADE, 1911. Two Edwardian ladies are enjoying a trip in a rowing boat, with the lock-keeper's cottage alongside the lock and the large boards showing the regulations to be observed on the river at this first lock on the Thames.

Inglesham Camp, Lechlade.

INGLESHAM CAMP, C. 1904. This picture has an unknown quality about it as although the tents are of army pattern, the deckchairs, dress and boats do anything but confirm the army connection!

INGLESHAM LOCK AND ROUNDHOUSE, C. 1903. The Thames and Severn Canal joined the River Thames in the centre of the picture at the point where the River Coln joined the Thames, coming in from the right. Initially the Canal Co. built a wharf, a lengthsman's cottage and a small warehouse here in 1789 as the terminal basin to the canal, but it proved unsuitable, and the company then purchased the established Parkend Wharf on the river at Lechlade in 1813. This wharf then became the base for the activities of the canal at this eastern end.

INGLESHAM CHURCH, C. 1910. The little church of St John the Baptist was declared redundant in 1979 and since 1981 it has been maintained by the Redundant Churches Fund. Its isolated location close by the River Thames, makes it well worth a visit for the undisturbed sixteenth-century atmosphere that still pervades with its carved oak screens and high pews.

FAIRFORD PARK HOUSE, c. 1910.

FAIRFORD PARK HOUSE GROUNDS, c. 1905. In the top view is the original three-storeyed mansion built in 1661 by Valentine Strong for Andrew Barker. Additions were made later in the eighteen century to both the house and the grounds. In 1955 the house was demolished and since 1961 Farmor's school has occupied the site. The Ernest Cook Trust, who bought the estate in 1945, retained the garages and the stable yard to the left for their offices. The grounds of the house were to the north and west of the house, and a glimpse of them is shown in the lower view. During the annual carnival held in Fairford these gardens were opened to the public.

FAIRFORD CHURCH, c. 1900. This classic view of the church of St Mary was used as a postcard view, and was on sale for about fifty years in different forms and finishes. The late Perpendicular-style church was rebuilt by John Tame and was finished by his son Sir Edmund Tame between 1480 and 1500. It is famous for its eight bells, its twenty-eight stained glass windows and its misericord seats, along with a whole host of other features, and it is visited by many tourists for these reasons. The windows are at present the subject of a very costly long-term restoration programme, which is aimed at protecting them for future generations to enjoy.

FAIRFORD CHURCH from the meadows, c. 1905.

A WINTER SCENE IN FAIRFORD, c. 1915. The River Coln flows through the town and many pictures taken include the river. The top view shows a lovely peaceful rural scene of the church from the water meadows alongside the river by Mill Bridge, while the lower view is taken further down the river looking across the small Bull Island towards the church. The building in front of the church is the rear of the Bull Tap public house.

The Market Place, Fairford.

FAIRFORD MARKET PLACE, C. 1908. There are only two bicycles in the whole of the Market Place and the High Street! On the right is the shop of E.B. Chew, family grocer and provision dealer, while next door is the Universal Stores of Green Bros, who were drapers, clothiers, hatters, hosiers and also sold toys, china, glass and earthenware, and no doubt hundreds of other small items too numerous to mention.

FAIRFORD HIGH STREET, 1907. This well-established line of shop fronts is almost unchanged today, but note how the large trees stretch far out over the road.

FAIRFORD MARKET, C. 1910. A market for animals became established in mid-Victorian times and was held on every second Tuesday in the month, but it eventually ceased trading just before the Second World War in the late 1930s. Sheep and pigs were penned with hurdles in the Market Place as seen here, while cattle were tethered further up the High Street and round into Park Street. There is a good crowd here mainly grouped by the auctioneer in his white smock at the far end of the pens. At the top of the High Street was a weighbridge at the side of the road for weighing the animals.

Bull Hotel, Fairford.

THE BULL HOTEL, FAIRFORD, c. 1930. The hotel dominates the Market Place and is thought to be mainly a seventeenth-century building and seen here under its plain tiled roof. The section at the far end was once the bank and the lower building to the left became the reading room. Earlier pictures show that the stonework was once plastered over but this was removed in the 1920s, and further alterations in the 1930s included a small porch over the old double coach doors under the sign, the construction of a low wall in front of the building and the insertion of dormer windows in the roof to match those of the bank building which was absorbed into the hotel after 1910, when the bank moved into its new premises in the High Street.

FAIRFORD MILL AND BRIDGE, 1903.

The Mill Pound, Fairford.

FAIRFORD MILL POND, C. 1916. The mill buildings seen in the top view are thought to date from the seventeenth century. The mill ceased to work as a corn mill around the start of the First World War. The buildings have been altered many times over the centuries and are now restored for accommodation. This scene has always been a very popular photograph. The lower view is taken from the ornamental bridge in the Park behind the mill and looks out across the mill pond and the overflow weir with the mill bridge in the centre and the water meadows in the distance.

THE MILL POND, FAIRFORD, c. 1907. Apart from the loss of trees this view is unchanged today. Note the two men trying their hand at fly fishing for trout in the pond.

TOWN BRIDGE, FAIRFORD, c. 1930. The garage selling Shell oils, Mobiloils and Pratts Motor Spirit was previously Constables Coach Works. The railings by the river were later replaced by a wall in 1947, and the little girl stands by the slope down into the river which was used as a watering place for animals, or for washing carts or for steam engines to take up water.

FAIRFORD FIRST AID PATROL, 1942. This is an official wartime photograph of the First Aid Patrol No. 53, and they had just been successful as the winners of the ARP Area and Divisional County Competition. Back row: A. Sandle, F. Law, W. Yells, A. Primmer. Front row: Miss Ironside, A.C. Goodman, leader, Miss Biltcliffe.

FAIRFORD HOSPITAL, c. 1900. This small cottage hospital was built in 1887 and was maintained by public subscription and funds raised by the annual carnival. In this view is the back of the hospital showing staff and patients.

H.R.H. *The Duke of Connaught & his Staff.*
Outside Bull Hotel, Fairford

HRH THE DUKE OF CONNAUGHT AT FAIRFORD, 1909. In 1909 the duke, who was the brother of King Edward VII and also Commander-in-Chief of the Army, brought two armies to the area for manoeuvres. The duke, seen here third from left, and his staff were accommodated at the Bull Hotel which had been suitably decorated with flags and plants for the occasion. W.D. Moss, with his royal patronage, was called out to Fairford to photograph this group, but other pictures of the troops on the move all over the district were taken by other local photographers such as C. Powell of Fairford and Davis of Lechlade.

MEYSEY HAMPTON VILLAGE, c. 1904. This shows the Green on which there were two water pumps, one at the top of some steps for filling farm watercarts and the other small hand pump for filling buckets. The Mason's Arms is just off the picture on the right and the Georgian facade of the Manor House can be seen by the trees on the right.

MEYSEY HAMPTON CHURCH, c. 1904. The cruciform church of St Mary is thought to have been built by the Knights Templar in the thirteenth century, but was restored in the 1870s by James Brooks who also carried out other work in the village, notably the school in 1872 and additions to the Rectory.

A PEEP IN POULTON, c. 1910.

LONDON ROAD, POULTON, c. 1930. These two similar views are of the main London road through the village and they show little change for the passing of twenty years. The top view shows some of the small stone-built cottages with Bell Lane going off northwards under the trees. By the 1930s, in the lower view, about twice as many telephone lines came through the village and the road has been tarred over.

THE NEW INN, POULTON, c. 1935. This inn was one of at least three known in the village but it was closed after the last war and is now a private house.

CRICKLADE STREET, POULTON, c. 1910.

The Falcon, Poulton.

POULTON VILLAGE, C. 1935. The A417 main road curves sharply down the hill to the left. The Falcon public house on the right sold Simmonds beers, while on the opposite side of the road is the late seventeenth-century Manor House built to a square pattern with its distinctive hipped roof.

The Vicarage, Poulton.

POULTON VICARAGE, 1911. A nicely proportioned, large stone-built house built by E. Christian in 1868.

The Ivy Church, Ampney St. Mary.

IVY CHURCH AT AMPNEY ST MARY, 1905. This small church of St Mary now stands isolated in the fields, the village having gradually disappeared from around it and re-establishing itself around the small community of Ashbrook when the coaching road was diverted away from the ford through the river after 1700. It has many surviving twelfth-century features and wall paintings thought to date back to the twelfth and fifteenth centuries.

AMPNEY ST PETER, 1905. The village is also known as Eastington. The building on the right later became the Packhorse Inn but has now been closed for some years. Most houses in the village are of well-preserved Cotswold stone, and the large village pond seen on the left backfilled with water from a ditch leading into the Ampney Brook. The small church of St Peter lies further up into the village and has some Saxon remains with a very low tower. It was restored by Sir G.G. Scott in 1878.

Ampney Crucis.

AMPNEY CRUCIS, C. 1910. The rest of the village is spread out along the road that bears left by the centre tree, but here on the main road the blacksmith's shop is on the left, while on the right one man is mending the stone wall and the other is digging out a soakaway for roadside water. In the distance are the original buildings of the Crown, now the much enlarged and very popular Crown of Crucis.

AMPNEY CRUCIS POST OFFICE, 1912. The post office was in this seventeenth-century house on the main road some distance from the rest of the village which is spread out up the lane. The small Ampney Brook runs under the road just up the lane.

View from the Bridge, Ampney Crucis.

THE GREEN, AMPNEY CRUCIS, 1912. Just behind the post office with the Upper Mill and church off to the left, where the large house is the Old Vicarage that partly dates back to the seventeenth century.

AMPNEY CRUCIS CHURCH, 1904. The church of the Holy Rood lies close to the wall of Ampney Park and it has interesting remains of Saxon and Norman work, as well as of other periods through to the nineteenth century, when it was restored in 1870. This restoration revealed wall paintings. Note the buildings of Ampney Park to the left of the tower and the churchyard cross which was restored in 1860, following the discovery of the head in a wall inside the church.

PRESTON CHURCH, 1904. The church of All Saints which was restored in 1862 has a good example of a fourteenth-century bellcote with three bells.

V. W. H. Cricklade Hounds at Kempsford.

VWH CRICKLADE HOUNDS MEET AT KEMPSFORD, C. 1913. The meet is seen here outside the George Inn. There is a large gathering of both huntsmen and onlookers, and they fill the road far into the distance so perhaps this was some special occasion.

KEMPSFORD VILLAGE, 1906.

KEMPSFORD VILLAGE, 1906. These two views of the High Street lead from one to the other. In the top view is the red-brick grocers and general shop, while in the lower view it is very evident how many thatched roofs existed in the village. Most of these cottages were built in the seventeenth or eighteenth centuries.

Kempsford Church.

KEMPSFORD CHURCH, 1904. The church of St Mary has fine Norman remains and a fine tower. The church was restored in the 1850s by G.E. Street, but the lychgate was added later in 1865 and other restoration was made after 1885.

CASTLE EATON CHURCH, 1905. The church of St Mary has Norman remains of c. 1170 with a bell turret and fifteenth-century tower.

MARSTON MEYSEY VICARAGE, 1905. The vicarage is opposite the church of St James which was built in 1875–77 by James Brooks. The painted glass windows in the church are by S.J. Bagally and were installed between 1883 and 1904.

DOWN AMPNEY VICARAGE, 1904. This was built in 1865 by E.J. Tarver and in 1872 Vaughan Williams, the composer, was born here when his father was the vicar. The low-roofed section at the far end is a chapel and this view of the house is exactly the same today in almost every detail, and no alterations have been made.

DOWN AMPNEY CHURCH, 1904. This large church of All Saints is mainly thirteenth century; it had a tall spire added in the fourteenth century, and a good porch added in the fifteenth century. The interior was restored in 1897 to incorporate much new carved woodwork.

DOWN AMPNEY CROSS, 1911. The village is largely made up of nineteenth-century cottages, but this cross is a copy of a fourteenth-century cross and was erected in 1878 at the eastern end of the village.

DOWN AMPNEY HOUSE LODGE, 1904. The house is fifteenth century and had alterations made to it in 1799 by Sir John Soane. This lodge or gatehouse leads into the Manor and is of the same Tudor period, but was burnt out in 1961 and finally demolished in 1963.

SECTION THREE
Cricklade to Tetbury

CRICKLADE HIGH STREET, 1905. Looking south along the road with St Mary's church on the right behind the tree. By the gas lamp opposite is the Red Lion public house. It is about where the horse and cart are situated that the northern line of the Saxon town wall crossed the road.

VWH CRICKLADE HOUNDS, 1910. The kennels for these hounds were between Meysey Hampton and Down Ampney, and the hounds are seen here at a local meet.

Cricklade Cattle Market.

CRICKLADE CATTLE MARKET, C. 1904. A very interesting picture full of action. The whole width of the High Street looking north is taken up with the animal market, and these markets continued up until the last war. In the foreground cattle are being herded away, while in the background a crowd has formed round the auctioneer down where the rest of the animals are penned. Note the large car in the middle of the road and although the names of the shops are difficult to make out, Carter is the first on the right and then Kempster next to the White Hart.

SOUTH CERNEY, 1902.

SOUTH CERNEY, 1902. These are two views of Silver Street. The top one is taken looking south and it well illustrates the small cottages of the eighteenth century with roses round their doors lining the road. Note the chapel in the distance and the horse-drawn rake coming up the road, possibly on its way to the blacksmith in School Lane. In the lower view, looking north, is the bridge over the River Churn and one of the village shops on the right.

SOUTH CERNEY CROSS, 1902. This village cross stands at the end of Silver Street where it meets Station Road and the High Street. The cross is unique with its stone ball and iron cross. The thatched cottage has long been demolished.

SIDDINGTON CHURCH, 1904. The church of St Peter has well-preserved Norman remains and was restored in 1864 by Woodyer when it is thought that the spire was added, along with other alterations. Church Farm buildings can just be seen over the hedges, but alas the huge old elm trees have gone now. The tythe barn of c. 1200 is at present the subject of restoration by English Heritage.

COVE HOUSE AT ASHTON KEYNES, 1905. Formerly the home of the Richmond family in the seventeenth-century, the house is off Fore Street. Note the gardener with the lawnmower and on the back of the card it says that a fete is to be held here. During the Second World War the house was used to billet troops on a short-term basis, but now the house is divided into two separate dwellings.

The Thames, Ashton Keynes.

THE RIVER THAMES AT ASHTON KEYNES, 1906. This is the mill race coming away from Ashton Mill with Church Walk on the right going down towards High Road. The view is almost unchanged today.

UPPER CROSS, Ashton Keynes, 1904.

A peep in Ashton Keynes.

A PEEP IN ASHTON KEYNES, 1904. The two views here almost join on to each other. The top one is along High Road with one of the four village crosses to the left and the bridge over the river. Note one of the village oil lamps at the junction. The building to the right has been demolished. In the lower view is the Long House with the River Thames running under the bridge and the water from the left coming from the mill. Note the cobbled slope alongside Church Walk and down into the river, probably for access for animals and carts to be washed and cleaned.

KENT END AT ASHTON KEYNES, 1904.

PARK PLACE, ASHTON KEYNES, 1907. In the distance is one of the village shops, and there is only one line on the telegraph pole, probably to the post office off to the left. The area of land to the right is now occupied by the garage of Ellisons Coaches.

MINETY CHURCH, 1905. The Perpendicular-style church of St Leonard.

BRAYDON HALL, MINETY, 1905. The house was built by George Pitt in 1751 facing Minety Common and was originally called Braydon or Pound House. Viscount and Lady Trafalgar lived there just after 1900 and later in 1925 Mr Fred Zeigler bought it, and enlarged and improved the property. Electric lights were installed and the generating plant was used up until 1947.

A PEEP IN MINETY, 1905. This is Moss's Corner in Upper Minety where the fork in the road goes left to Hankerton. The buildings in the centre are now known as the Old Toll House, but in the late nineteenth century it was the post office with the shoeing forge at the back. The blacksmith was Moss and it was also possible to hire horses, carts and traps.

POOLE KEYNES, 1904. A small parish which was transferred from Wiltshire to Gloucestershire in 1897. The top of the cross is now missing and the barn to the right has been converted to a house.

MALMESBURY FIRE ENGINE, 1902. This is the old parish fire engine. It would have been dragged along to the fire and then pumped by six men, three at each set of handles. The leather buckets were used to carry water to put into the cistern of the pump, and a fireman would have stood on top and directed the jet of water on to the fire.

MALMESBURY MARKET CROSS, 1903. Without doubt this is one of the finest such crosses in the country. It has eight sides and is over 40 feet high, having been built around 1500.

A DELIVERY LORRY, C. 1915. A new Ford lorry supplied to Stephen Pettifer & Sons Ltd, who were dealers in animal medical treatments for a considerable area around Malmesbury.

MALMESBURY ABBEY, 1906. The ruins of the Abbey dominate the town with the Abbot's House to the left. The Abbey was founded in the seventh century and became famous for its shrine of St Aldhelm. After the dissolution the nave was saved to become the parish church with nineteenth-century restoration helping to preserve the building which had been allowed to deteriorate for many centuries. Note the railway line and level crossing in the front of the picture. This was a $6\frac{1}{2}$ mile long branch line from the GWR at Dauntsey, but later in the 1930s it was shortened from the Badminton line when a new junction was created at Somerford. In 1946 there were seven trains each way each day.

CRUDWELL VILLAGE, 1903. This is the Malmesbury Road into Crudwell with the Wheatsheaf on the left. The small donkey cart seems to be well loaded with children.

CRUDWELL VILLAGE, 1903. This is now the Mayfield Hotel taken from the bridge out in the road to Cirencester and here called the Street. The hotel is much altered with the verandah gone, and also the thatched cottage opposite has been demolished.

Kemble House.

KEMBLE HOUSE, 1904. The 120 ft high spire of the church of All Saints rises over the roof of Kemble House. The church was almost completely rebuilt in 1872–8 by Medland & Son, except the tower and the spire. The House or Manor House is seventeenth century, but altered in the nineteenth and twentieth centuries and is now sometimes used for exhibitions.

A Part of Kemble Village.

KEMBLE VILLAGE, 1905. This little road is School Lane leading down to the school which can be seen in the background. Opposite the school is the village hall, built in the same style as the school in 1899.

Blacksmith's Shop and Cottage, Kemble.

THE BLACKSMITH'S SHOP, KEMBLE, 1904. The blacksmith was in Church Road and the sign over the door is 'H. Gascoign RSS by Examination & General Smith'. Note the farm machinery for repair in the yard to the left. Behind the shop is the cemetery with graves dating back to the 1880s.

A Peep in Kemble.

KEMBLE VILLAGE, 1904. The stone arch was built over the village pump in the centre of the village by the green. The road left is West Lane while the road to the right has now been closed to traffic.

THE COFFEE TAVERN, KEMBLE, c. 1908. This is now the Tavern public house with the railway station off to the right. It is thought that the Coffee Tavern was built c. 1890 as the refreshment rooms for the new station built in 1886 after the Tetbury branch line was added at Kemble, as there had never been any refreshment rooms at the station. Prior to this date the main line station was further up the line on the Tetbury Road.

THE RIVER THAMES AT KEMBLE, 1904. In the background is the 1841 branch line to Cirencester, and it passes over the road at the same time as the River Thames crosses under the road, and is sometimes referred to as the first bridge over the Thames. That is not strictly true as there is a bridge under the Fosse Way on the Tetbury Road, but of course there is not always water there.

KEMBLE WICK, 1904. This tiny hamlet is on the Oaksey Road into Kemble. The cottages on the left have been demolished and a more modern house built on the site. The Wiltshire and Gloucestershire boundary, and also parish boundaries, come through the hamlet and the names of the houses reflect this division.

BETWEEN KEMBLE AND EWEN, 1903. Apart from the loss of the large trees the view is almost unchanged along this road. The small River Thames crosses under the road at Parkers Bridge in the middle distance by the lady with the pram.

Cook's Cottage, Ewen Road.

COOK'S COTTAGE along the Kemble Road, 1904.

COTTAGES IN EWEN, 1903. These old cottages, now called Thursday Cottage, stood on the corner where Peastones Lane goes off to Siddington, and the road on the right curves to South Cerney. There was a lot of thatch used in this village, some of which has survived today.

EWEN VILLAGE, 1904. This small lane runs through at the back of the present Wild Duck Inn and some of their buildings are on the right. The other cottages further down have been greatly altered. Note the different types of roof in the picture – clay tiles, Cotswold stone tiles, slates and thatch.

Tetbury to Birdlip

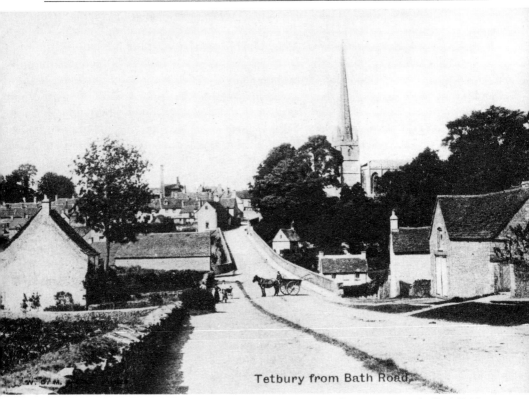

Tetbury from Bath Road.

TETBURY FROM THE BATH ROAD, 1904. This approach road into the town is over the Bath Bridge built in 1775 for the turnpike commissioners. In the centre can be seen the tall chimney of Warn's Brewery, while the tall elegant spire of St Mary's church dominates the scene. The church was rebuilt in the Gothic style by Francis Hiorn in the late eighteenth century.

The Town Hall, Tetbury.

TETBURY TOWN HALL, 1909. The Town Hall or Market House was perhaps used in connection with the wool trade. It was built in 1655 with its upper floor supported on short, thick stone pillars. Alterations were made to it in 1817. Note the White Hart Hotel, behind which was rebuilt in the mid-nineteenth century.

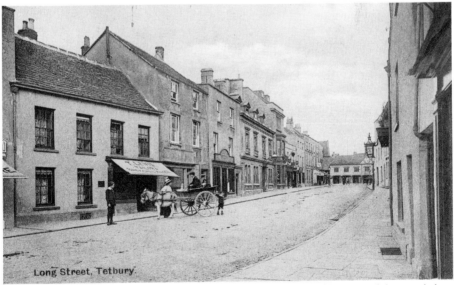

Long Street, Tetbury.

LONG STREET, TETBURY, 1909. This is the view towards the Market House, and the good shop frontages reflect the wealth of the wool merchants of the time when the town was the wool collection centre for the surrounding area. Note the shop of T. Lewis, Tailors & Breeches Maker, with the donkey cart outside and the early garage business midway along the street.

Long Street, Tetbury, from the Market.

LONG STREET, TETBURY, c. 1910.

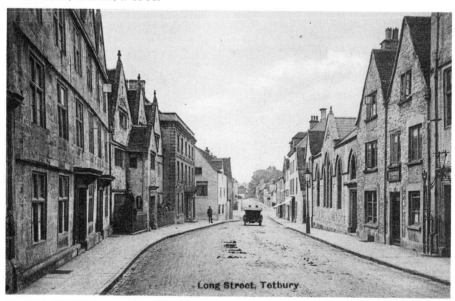

Long Street, Tetbury.

LONG STREET, TETBURY, c. 1910. These two views virtually join on to each other. The top view is from the Market House. On the left is the Stationery, Toy and Fancy Repository of J. Clark with an elegant lamp-post outside, while opposite is the grocery and provision shop of Fawkes and the Pent House Tea Rooms. In the lower view is the extension towards the crossroads which once more shows the good frontages to the street with the two-storeyed porch of Porch House on the left.

AT WESTONBIRT HOUSE, C. 1920. Her Majesty Queen Mary honoured Sir George and Lady Holford with a visit to Westonbirt House. The queen is standing second left by the 9th Duke of Beaufort and Sir George Holford is in the centre with his hands on his lapels. The Marquess of Worcester, who later became the 10the Duke of Beaufort, is on horseback on the right. The Duke of Beaufort's hounds visited the house during the queen's stay at Westonbirt.

WESTONBIRT SCHOOL, C. 1935. Built as Westonbirt House in the late nineteenth century by Lewis Vulliamy for R.S. Holford in the Elizabethan style. In 1928 the estate was sold and a trust set up the present girls school. This view of the gardens shows the extensive grounds around the school which stands in fine wooded parkland.

THE HARE AND HOUNDS HOTEL, WESTONBIRT, C. 1925. The old coaching inn on the main road was pulled down by order of R.S. Holford and rebuilt in 1854 on its present site. The whole village had gradually been moved away from the church and rebuilt farther to the west away from the site of the proposed Westonbirt House.

RODMARTON CHURCH, 1912. The church of St Peter has surviving features from the thirteenth century and was restored twice in Victorian times in 1862 and later in 1884.

RODMARTON ESTATE LORRY, C. 1915. This International lorry was supplied by Bridges the Agricultural Engineers of Whiteway Works, Cirencester to the Rodmarton Estate of the Hon. C. Biddulph. Rodmarton Manor was built by Ernest Barnsley between 1909 and 1926 for the Hon. Claud Biddulph using traditional local materials and craftsmen from the estate.

Thames Head. The true Source of the Thames.

THAMES HEAD, 1914. The source of the River Thames can be reached by walking across the fields to Trewsbury Mead from Coates, or from the Tetbury road. But it is only after prolonged periods of wet weather in the winter and early spring that water issues from the spring. Controversy still reigns about this spring being the source of the Thames; the source of the River Churn, a main tributary of the Thames lies further away and issues water for longer periods. Behind the old ash tree and up on the bank lies the Thames and Severn Canal and some years ago the statue of Old Father Thames had to be removed from here to St John's Lock at Lechlade following vandalism. Now there is only a granite stone proclaiming this to be the source of the Thames.

Tunnel House.

TUNNEL HOUSE, COATES, 1906. Originally called the New Inn, this was built in the late eighteenth century by the Canal Co. to house men working in the canal tunnel. It is seen here as a public house in the latter days of the canal's working life when Joseph Norton was landlord and licensed to sell beer, ale, porter and cider. The building was badly damaged by fire in 1952 and was subsequently rebuilt without its top floor which gave the building a completely different roof line. Substantial internal alterations were also made at this time.

Trewsbury House, Coates.

TREWSBURY HOUSE, COATES, 1912. This house is built within the Iron Age hill fort at Trewsbury about half a mile north-west of the Fosse Way at Thames Head.

Dockem House, Coates.

DOCKEM HOUSE, COATES, 1912. Built by V.A. Lawson before the First World War. Note the tennis court to the left and the croquet lawns in the foreground.

A Part of Coates, Nr. Cirencester.

COATES VILLAGE, 1912. This is Setts Road leading off The Street. The cottage in the distance has been much altered and extended, and is now called Coates House, while other houses called Setts Row have been built in the field on the left.

The Street, Coates, Nr. Cirencester.

THE STREET, COATES, 1912. Looking towards the main Cirencester-to-Stroud road with the school buildings of 1849 on the right. The school is now closed and the premises are for sale. Cottages on the left have been demolished and the area is now known as Bathurst Row.

QUAKERS ROW, 1912. Otherwise known as the 'Row of Ten', these cottages were for the estate workers on Coates Manor. In the last few years the area has been developed and now modern houses fill the large gardens hiding Quakers Row from the road. One pair of the cottages at the end was demolished to allow access for the new development.

THE STROUD VALLEY AT CHALFORD, 1912. The houses of Chalford tumble down the steep slope of the River Frome valley and prominent in the bottom is the Thames and Severn Canal with Clowes Lock in the centre. Above the lock is the large complex of Seville's Mill. Up on the slope to the right is the GWR line with Chalford signal box and the rail-motor shed in the distance.

THE BRIMSCOMBE VALLEY, 1904. A wide panoramic view up the valley, but details in the picture are difficult to see. The road, railway and canal are all brought close together here and in the centre is Brimscombe station. Lewiston Mill with its tall chimney is to the left and Brimscombe Gas Works to the right with the complex of buildings just over the trees being the Bourne Saw Mills.

CHESS AND STEAD LTD, BRIMSCOMBE, c. 1920. A new International lorry as supplied to Chess and Stead, who were manufacturers of rubber materials at Lower Mills in Brimscombe.

DICKINSON & COX, COAL AND COKE MERCHANTS, STROUD AND STONEHOUSE, c. 1920. Coal is being unloaded into bushel baskets in their International lorry AD 8875. The coal wagon they are emptying has come from British Coppice Colliery via the Kingsbury Junction on the Midland Railway near Sutton Coldfield. Note the railway yard crane in the background. This photograph is from the period when W.D. Moss had a working relationship with the photographer Peckham in Stroud.

ARUNDEL MILL, STROUD, C. 1920. The International lorry here belonged to Gyde Bishop & Co. at Arundel Mill. It is loaded with sacks of wool for dyeing and is in the mill yard.

High Street, Stonehouse.

STONEHOUSE HIGH STREET, 1904. This view is looking north-west along the High Street towards Gloucester. Regent Street lies off to the left and the area to the right behind the iron fence is now occupied by the post office and other shops. Most of the buildings further along the street are still there.

THE BEAR HOTEL, AMBERLEY, 1909.

THE BEAR HOTEL GARDENS, AMBERLEY, 1909. These pictures show the original seventeenth century buildings before the extensions of the 1920s which dwarfed the original buildings. In the top view a board underneath the Bear sign proclaims the hotel to be the headquarters of the Stroud Golf Club and the Rodborough Bowling Club, and the galvanized iron Stroud Golf Club building is to the left, probably painted in stripes to look more like a marquee. The Golf Club was established in the early 1900s and by 1906 had a nine-hole course on Rodborough Common. They held their first meeting in 1907 at their new clubhouse, but by 1930 both the Stroud and Rodborough clubs had folded, while Minchinhampton Club, established in 1889, carried on at their course on Minchinhampton Common.

GEORGE STREET, Nailsworth, 1904. This is the view towards the Nailsworth 'W' and Minchinhampton Common. Most of the buildings shown still remain except that the tall house beyond the George Hotel has been developed and is now the Midland Bank. The hotel, which was closed in the late 1980s and was to be demolished, was saved by local protests, but remains boarded up.

FOUNTAIN STREET, Nailsworth, 1904. This view down the street into the town is almost unchanged. The wooden clock tower was built to house the clock from the 1794 Anglican church that stood on the site of the present St George's parish church on the right. St George's was built in 1898, but the tower was never built and the clock was temporarily housed in the wooden tower. This tower was pulled down in 1952 and the clock transferred to the stone tower in the centre of the town by George Street. Note the horse bus going down the hill and the lack of trees up on the Common

DANEWAY HOUSE, c. 1930. This fine Cotswold manor house dates mainly from the mid-fourteenth century but the five-storeyed gabled tower dates from the early seventeenth century, and there have been no further major alterations to the buildings since 1717. There are early references to the house in 1339, and it was used by the Hancox family for almost 500 years up to 1860. It was sold to Earl Bathurst in 1897 who then commissioned Ernest Barnsley to restore it. In 1902 Ernest Barnsley and Ernest Gimson were allowed to move from Pinbury Park with their furniture workshops and showroom, and in conjunction with other locally-based craftsmen the Arts and Crafts movement flourished. Following Gimson's death in 1919, the house passed into private ownership and the remaining craftsmen moved to the Silk Mill at Chalford under the guidance of Peter Waals.

Sapperton Village

SAPPERTON VILLAGE, 1904. This view along Top Road shows the village overlooking the deep valley of the River Frome. The stone cottages have been built mainly since the seventeenth century, and now even the newer ones tend to look old and blend in with the older ones. In the middle distance it is possible to see the end elevation of the school.

Sapperton School & Village.

SAPPERTON SCHOOL, 1904. A lovely bright scene looking towards the church with the school on the left. Lord Bathurst gave this school to the village in 1848 and just past the building is the lane down to the Lower Road. Note Shep Allen, the shepherd from Manor Farm, with his bundle of wood under his arm. It was necessary for most people to collect a bundle of wood each day so that they could have a fire the next day.

St. Kenelm's Church, Sapperton.

SAPPERTON CHURCH, 1904. The cruciform church of St Kenelm stands on the site of an earlier Norman church and was largely rebuilt in the fourteenth century with other alterations in later centuries. It contains fine monuments to Sir Henry Poole and his family, and to Sir Robert Atkyns. In 1934 the spire was repaired and while the weather-cock was down on the ground the local children were able to 'jump over the weather-cock'.

SAPPERTON VILLAGE HALL, 1912. The hall was designed by Ernest Barnsley and Norman Jewson, craftsmen at Daneway House, and it was built in traditional Cotswold style with gabled roof and mullioned windows. The photograph shows the newly completed building which was later furnished with craftsman-made chairs and tables, and this furniture still exists today.

The Bell, Sapperton.

THE BELL, SAPPERTON, 1904.

The Nuns' Walk, Pinbury Park.

PINBURY PARK, C. 1905. The Park was the home of Sir Robert Atkyns until his death in 1711 and the craftsman Ernest Barnsley renovated the house for Earl Bathurst and used the outbuildings for furniture workshops prior to moving to Daneway House in 1902. The Nuns Walk is within the grounds of the house and is said to be haunted by the ghost of a nun.

DAGLINGWORTH, C. 1920. This view towards the south-east across the village shows the road back to Stratton and the church of the Holy Rood up on the higher ground on the right. The church has typical Saxon long and short work, and an inscribed Roman stone has been converted to a window. The ground behind the house to the right was once allotments but has recently been built upon. The small River Dun flows through the meadows on the left.

DAGLINGWORTH RECTORY, C. 1905. This large house was rebuilt by James Piers St Aubyn in 1856 in the thirteenth century style with large, banded-brick chimneys.

FARM COURT, DAGLINGWORTH, C. 1900.

FARM COURT, DAGLINGWORTH, 1935. These two views could almost be entitled 'then and now'. Both views are at the crossroads with the lane up to the church behind the camera. The small Dun stream crosses under the road by the end terraced cottage on the left. Geoffrey Scrutton, who owned most of the village, made extensive alterations, and also demolished properties in the village. The alterations seen here are typical of that period and the cottages have been changed almost beyond recognition. In the top view the village stores were in the house on the right and the blacksmith's was just up the lane where the horse is standing.

DUNTISBOURNE ROUSE CHURCH, 1904. This little church of St Michael is built into the steep slope of the valley and is of great interest because it was not restored to any degree in the nineteenth century, and has remained unaltered since the seventeenth century. The nave is thought to be Saxon and has long and short quoin work and herring-bone masonry, while the chancel and the crypt beneath it are of the Norman period. The small saddleback tower at the western end is dated 1587 and the churchyard cross is fourteenth century and retains part of the original head on its slender shaft.

MISERDEN HOUSE, 1904. Otherwise known as Misarden Park, it was built in the early seventeenth century and altered extensively in 1875 by Alfred Waterhouse. This picture predates the extension that was built in 1914 by Andrew Russell that was destroyed by fire in 1919. Another extension was then built in 1921 by Sir Edwin Lutyens.

MISERDEN VILLAGE, 1903. This is the centre of the village with the Carpenters Arms to the right and the typical estate houses on the left which date from the mid-Victorian period, around 1860. The first house on the left, Russell Cottage, 1867, was the village post office.

SECTION FIVE

Birdlip to Northleach

THE ROYAL GEORGE HOTEL, BIRDLIP, 1906.

THE ROYAL GEORGE HOTEL GARDENS, BIRDLIP, 1904. The village lies on the line of the old Roman Ermin Street and the hotel is at the top of the famous steep Birdlip Hill. Since the hotel was built in the nineteenth century it was been a most convenient and welcome place to stop. An interesting notice at the left-hand end of the hotel announces petrol for sale from the City Garage Ltd and one of the early cars among this meet of the Cotswold Hounds has the registration number AD 110. The hotel had extensive grounds at the rear looking out over the steep edge of the Cotswolds, and Edwardian ladies took tea there in the summerhouses, as seen in the lower view.

BIRDLIP VILLAGE, C. 1915. This road used to carry all the main road traffic from Gloucester to Cirencester, but since the opening of the Birdlip bypass this has now become a quiet village again and it is almost possible to stand in the road here once more. Note the fingerpost sign to Brimpsfield on the right, just in front of Birdlip House Farm. On the left are the school buildings with the bellcote and this is still Birdlip County Primary School with extra classrooms at the rear.

BIRDLIP MISSION CHURCH, 1914. This building is now gone but the large house opposite still remains along a footpath on the Witcombe Estate just off the Stroud road out of Birdlip.

THE LILLEY BROOK HOTEL, CHARLTON KINGS, c. 1920. The house that stood on this site burnt down in 1831 and it was rebuilt in the 1840s with later additions in the 1890s. The stables which have been recently converted to a restaurant may have been from the original house. Shortly after the First World War it became the Lilley Brook Hotel and this may explain why W.D. Moss took this picture, perhaps to celebrate that occasion. Various local events took place here such as meets of the hounds, fetes, and Red Cross exercises and the hotel became a favourite place to stay with golfing enthusiasts on the adjacent course. The hotel closed in the late 1970s, but since has been handsomely restored and has re-opened as the Cheltenham Park Hotel.

SEVEN SPRINGS, 1902. These springs are the source of the River Churn and are just over the top of Charlton Kings Hill up out of Cheltenham. It became a favourite spot for Edwardian outings and picnics, and the message on this postcard confirms this point and merely says 'The Picnic Spot'. The springs are regarded by some people as the source of the River Thames rather than the spring at Thames Head, and no doubt this argument will always be put forward.

ELKSTONE CHURCH, 1905. The church of St John the Evangelist is well known for its outstanding Norman features. The church retains its Norman plan and has fine arches and south doorway. The original central tower probably collapsed in the thirteenth century and the opportunity was taken to raise the roof when the space created was adapted as a Columbarium with holes for pigeons to nest. The present west tower is a fine example of the perpendicular style of the fifteenth century.

THE COLESBOURNE INN, C. 1925. The Colesbourne was built in 1827 alongside the 1825 turnpike road as a typical stopping place and horse changeover station for the coaches. The design had ashlar quoins, three gables and Cotswold stone-tiled roof, and a matching block of stables just off this picture to the left. Some years ago these stables were converted to become part of the Inn.

NORTH CERNEY CHURCH, 1905. The twelfth century church of All Saints is built on the site of a much earlier church. It has Norman remains but has been altered over the centuries. Its present beautiful state is due to the generosity of W.I. Croome and the details to be found in the fabric of the building can only be appreciated by visiting the church.

RENDCOMB PARK, C. 1915. This is the view of Rendcomb Park from the main road. The buildings were designed in the Italianate style by Philip Hardwick for Sir F.H. Goldsmith and were built by Thomas Cubitt in 1863. The site had previously been occupied by the sixteenth-century manor house of Sir Christopher Guise and this was demolished in order to build Rendcomb Park. Since 1920 the house has been a school and college founded by F.N.H. Wills.

RENDCOMB CHURCH AND RECTORY, c. 1925.

A PEEP IN RENDCOMB, 1912. The River Churn valley is very wooded here as can be seen in the top view. Both pictures show the church of St Peter which was entirely rebuilt in the perpendicular style at the beginning of the sixteenth century by John Tame who had previously rebuilt Fairford church, and it has been suggested that some of the stained glass used in the windows was the surplus left from the windows at Fairford. The Old Rectory, a typical symmetrical Georgian building, is now used by the college.

BAUNTON CHURCH, C. 1935. The small church of St Mary Magdalene has Norman origins but has been altered a great deal over the centuries. During restoration in 1877 a remarkable, large well-preserved fourteenth century wall painting of St Christopher was uncovered. St Christopher is shown with a long staff and wading through water which is full of fish.

Badgendon Church, Glos.

BAGENDON CHURCH AND VILLAGE, 1906. The little church of St Margaret has Norman remains, especially in the lower tower which has a saddle-back roof. A small tributary of the River Churn crosses under the road in front of the church and sometimes this area flooded, so in medieval times the floors inside the building were raised. It was restored in Victorian times in 1889 by S. Gambier-Parry. This scene is very little changed today.

LowerChedworth.

LOWER CHEDWORTH, 1925. This is the view across the lower end of the village towards Stowell Park on the horizon. Prominent in the picture is the pyramidal slate roof of the 1804 Congregational chapel. Mr M. Perry, the village grocer, is seen in the foreground, and W.D. Moss produced a series of seventeen postcards for him to sell, and this view plus the next three are part of that series.

Middle Chedworth. 13.

MIDDLE CHEDWORTH, 1925. This is looking down the valley towards Fossebridge. It shows the railway line of the GWR which was made into a double track in 1902. This line was previously known as the Midland and South Western Junction and it ran from Andover to Andoversford. In the village almost every house is built of Cotswold stone, but there appears to be all manner of roofing from Cotswold stone tiles, to thatch, slates, clay tiles and even corrugated iron.

CHEDWORTH VILLAGE, 1925. Another view towards Fossebridge with the railway line almost concealed behind the clump of trees on the right. The house in the foreground was enlarged to become the police station and the cottages above it are known as the Rookery.

CHURCH ROW, CHEDWORTH, 1925. These cottages date from the eighteenth century and are opposite the church, note the tombstones in the foreground. Just down the hill on the right is the Seven Tuns, one of the two village inns of the day.

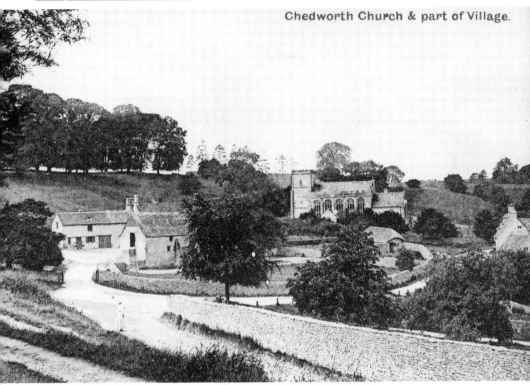

CHEDWORTH CHURCH AND VILLAGE, 1904. This shows the church of St Andrews and Manor Farm to the left with the area that was once the centre of the early village. That area was behind the branches of the copper beech tree where the tythe barn once stood. This barn was demolished a few years before this photograph was taken. The scene remains virtually unchanged today, except for tree growth. The church is of the late Norman period with its original plan, but it was considerably altered in the fifteenth century and also when it was restored in 1883.

CHEDWORTH ROMAN VILLA MUSEUM, 1904.

Nº 3. Roman Villa. Chedworth.

CHEDWORTH ROMAN VILLA, 1912. The villa was discovered in 1864 and the top view shows the original 1865 museum building on the left which was started soon after the excavations at the site began. The house on the right was added a little later as accommodation for Lord Eldon's employees. It was also used as a shooting lodge on the estate and was usually occupied by the estate buildings and maintenance foreman. In the lower view is the western half of the northern wing of the excavated villa showing the pillars which supported the floor of the heated room. An interesting point about this postcard, and some others in the series on the villa, is that they sold in some thousands per year to the visitors to the villa and museum for decades.

WITHINGTON VILLAGE, C. 1935. The photographs on this and the next page go together as they are part of a series taken at the same time. This view shows the crossroads with the road going straight on to Cheltenham.

WITHINGTON VILLAGE, c. 1935. The road to Colesbourne. Note the predominance of creepers on the buildings in both pictures and the tower of St Michael's church above the roofs. The church contains interesting work of all periods from Norman through to Perpendicular, but it was drastically restored in 1872 by David Brandon.

THE MILL INN, Withington, 1914. This shows the very popular inn with the roof of the corn mill buildings in the trees to the right. As with the two previous Withington pictures, the building is covered with creepers. The gardens in the foreground were separated from the inn by the road which comes close to the front of the buildings.

ACKNOWLEDGEMENTS

Our first thanks go to Mrs D. Allen, the daughter of W. Dennis Moss, whose help enabled us to make the Introduction as correct as possible.

We are also grateful to the following people for the information that was so freely given to us which helped us to caption many of the photographs:

Cirencester Park Polo Club
Mr S. Gardiner
Mr N. Irvine
Mrs G. Lock
Mr W. Tindle
Mr D. Viner, Curator of the Corinium Museum

INDEX